ANCIENT GREECE

Miguel Ángel Saura

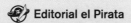 Editorial el Pirata

KEY POINTS IN THE HISTORY OF ANCIENT GREECE

3400 BC
Birth of the
Minoan civilization

17th-11th centuries BC
Mycenae and the
Dorian invasions

Approximately
13th century BC
The Trojan War

1st century BC-6th century AD
The fall of Hellenism

12th-8th centuries BC
The Dark Ages

5th-4th centuries BC
The Classical Period

776 BC
The first Olympic
Games

4th-1st centuries BC
The Hellenistic Period

5th century BC
The Greco-Persian Wars

CONTENTS

WHO WERE THE GREEKS?

The history of the Greeks started very early. No sooner had the region emerged from prehistoric times than great civilizations evolved that knew about writing, created interesting works of art, and built impressive palaces. These cultures disappeared, swept away by invasions, in what is known as the **Dark Ages**.

After this period of wars and destruction, Greek culture began to appear. This was the **Archaic Period**, which ended when the Greeks defeated the Persians. It was then that the **Classical Period** began, during which their civilization reached its full glory. This cultural golden age ended with Macedonia's invasion of Greece. **The Hellenistic Period** was the age in which Greek culture expanded into Asia, and it ended with the Roman conquest of Greece and Macedonia, following which the Greeks became subjects of the Roman Empire.

Greece is a **small, mountainous** country. Its rugged landscape and steep roads made overland communication very difficult. The Greeks never bothered to build good roads, and fertile, easily cultivated land was on the rare side. So, from the beginning, Greek cities depended on **trade** for survival. The mountainous terrain isolated the population, so that while they belonged to a single people, the Greeks of various regions were very different from each other. They could never agree for long enough to create empires as large as those of the Egyptians and Persians.

However, the Greek coastline is dotted with beaches and natural harbors. In fact, almost every city was near the coast and had its own harbor. This meant that the Greeks, as a people, had a very close relationship with the **sea**.

Greek **merchants** sailed all over the Mediterranean in search of buyers for their amphorae of oil and wine. When the ships returned from their voyages, they brought back to their cities Egyptian medicine, Persian science, and Phoenician navigation techniques, to name just a few examples.

Their civilization was always open to new ideas, and they took art, culture, and science much further than any other people in the ancient world.

MACEDONIA

MOUNT
OLYMPUS

AEGEAN SEA

PERSIA

IONIA

THERMOPYLAE
THEBES

MARATHON

CORINITH

ATHENS

SALAMIS

OLYMPIA

SPARTA

MEDITERRANEAN SEA

CRETE

THE MINOAN CIVILIZATION

The first great culture of the area appeared on **Crete**, an island just south of Greece. It is known as the Minoan culture because its most legendary king was called **Minos**. It lasted from around 3400 to 1200 BC.

In those times, the Cretans dominated the Mediterranean thanks to a powerful **war fleet** that protected their merchant ships.

When civilization began to develop on mainland Greece, the Greeks tried to imitate Minoan art and culture.

The Cretans built impressive **palaces** of several stories high, with terraces and inner courtyards. The walls were decorated with paintings depicting the Cretan people enjoying an elegant and sophisticated way of life.

No one knows when or why the Minoan civilization **disappeared**, but it may have been due to a series of natural disasters, such as earthquakes, volcano eruptions, or tsunamis, followed by an invasion.

YOU MAY NOT KNOW THAT...

Bulls were sacred animals to the Minoans. They can be found everywhere on Cretan archeological sites: statuettes of bulls, medallions with bulls, sculptures of bulls... Even the Minoan city walls are decorated with horns. But the most spectacular representations are the **wall paintings**, which depict a curious ritual.

The paintings show boys and girls jumping and dancing around these animals. These rituals took place in the inner courtyards of the palaces, some of which were up to four stories high. Crete's magnificent palaces, as seen through the eyes of the much more primitive Greeks of the time, were probably the origin of the legend of the **Minotaur**'s labyrinth.

The Minotaur

Legend has it that the king of Crete, **Minos**, was unable to have children and asked the gods for help. The god of the sea, **Poseidon**, sent him a magnificent **white bull** to sacrifice in his honor, but Minos kept the bull and sacrificed another animal instead. When Poseidon realized, he was very angry and made Pasiphae, the King's wife, fall in love with the bull. A few months later, the queen gave birth to a monstrous baby, half-man and half-bull: the **Minotaur**.

The child grew up to become a cruel, savage being that fed on people. Horrified, Minos ordered the famous architect **Daedalus** to design a place to imprison the monster—a construction so complex that it was impossible to get out once you had gone in. They called it a **labyrinth**.

Then war broke out between the Greek city of Athens and the Cretans, led by Minos. Crete won the war, and Minos demanded a terrible condition in exchange for peace: Every year, Athens would send ten boys and ten girls to Crete to be devoured by the Minotaur.

The king of Greece's son, **Theseus**, volunteered to kill the monster. Minos' daughter, **Ariadne**, fell in love with Theseus and gave him two gifts:

a sword so he could defend himself against the monster and a **spool of yarn** to tie at the entrance and unwind as he went deeper into the labyrinth. So, after slaying the Minotaur, Theseus was able to find his way back thanks to Ariadne's thread and return to Athens victorious.

The Flight of Icarus

When the labyrinth was finished, **Daedalus** sent the bill to King Minos. When the king saw the price, he decided to save the money by **enclosing** Daedalus and his son, **Icarus**, in the labyrinth to be the Minotaur's dinner.

Daedalus, lost in the prison that he himself had built, found an old eagle's nest full of feathers. He made **wings** out of them, using beeswax to attach the feathers to a wooden structure that he invented. When the two sets of wings were ready, father and son left the labyrinth by air, and they flew off home over the sea. Before they set off, Daedalus warned his son not to fly too high, but Icarus didn't listen to his father; he was too enthusiastic about flying. He flew so high that the heat of the **sun** melted the wax, and the feathers came unstuck, causing Icarus to fall into the sea and drown.

By the time Minoan culture had disappeared, a new civilization was emerging in mainland Greece: the **Mycenean** civilization, lasting from around 1700 to 1050 BC. These were no longer primitive peoples but complete societies with palaces and fortresses that dominated large regions. The entire country was divided up into small kingdoms which were all at war with each other, each led by a king and a group of elite warriors with weapons made of bronze.

Peasants and slaves cultivated the land. The crops were stored in huge, fortified **palaces** where the king and the nobles lived. These palaces had mighty walls, storerooms, and houses that were several stories high.

Mycenaean culture was strongly influenced by Minoan culture. Some experts believe that the Mycenaean warriors had something to do with the demise of Minoan civilization. The Mycenaeans may have taken advantage of a natural disaster to **attack** the Cretan cities, which didn't have city walls around them because they relied on their powerful battle fleet to protect them from invasion.

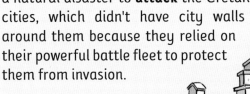

Combat Chariots

At that time, the hardest known material was **bronze**, a mixture of copper and tin. It's a tough, resistant metal that is easy to shape. However, tin was very **expensive** and scarce, so only the really **rich** could afford the most sophisticated military equipment: bronze swords, shields, and amour, as well as **war chariots** pulled by a pair of horses.

These chariots were the state-of-the-art technology of the time: fast and sturdy, they carried a **two-man** crew. One was the **driver**, who steered the horses against the enemy formation, and the other was the **marksman**, who threw arrows and javelins at the enemy and could run away quickly when they counter-attacked.

Mycenaean civilization lasted about **seven hundred** years, until alliances of northern tribes, the **Dorians**, came on the scene. The Dorians were part of a wave of invading peoples who came to Europe from the east in search of fertile land. The Dorian peoples destroyed the Mycenaean civilization between the 12th and 11th centuries BC, burning their palaces and killing or enslaving much of the population.

With them came what is known as the **Dark Ages**, a period of several centuries in which various peoples turned to plunder and piracy, leading to the fall of the great civilizations of the Mediterranean region.

The Cyclopean Walls

Greeks from later periods came across the remains of Mycenaean palaces and were pretty amazed, especially because the walls were built with massive **stones** which were carefully carved and fitted together to a fraction of an inch, as if they were the pieces of a puzzle.

Near these ruined walls, they found gigantic **skulls**, each with a large hole in its forehead. The Greeks thought they must have been the remains of one-eyed giants, and so the idea of **Cyclopes**, who often appear in their mythology, was born. To them, it made sense to think that Cyclopes had built the Mycenaean walls. In architecture, walls built with large blocks of stone are still called **Cyclopean walls**.

The skulls that the Greeks found actually belonged to a species of **elephant** that had lived all along the Mediterranean coast. They were smaller than African elephants, but their skulls were still much bigger than a person's. The **hollow** in the middle of the forehead wasn't the eye socket but the spot where the trunk muscles joined the skull.

You can't deny that the Ancient Greeks had very good **imaginations**.

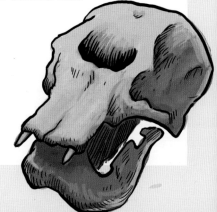

THE DARK AGES

12th-8th Centuries BC

Toward the end of the Bronze Age, the last Prehistoric Period, a terrible **volcanic eruption** filled the atmosphere with dust, and crops failed all over the world. Famine displaced large numbers of people from the Black Sea area to Greece, Italy, and the Middle East, who plundered the villages in their path. In Greece's case, bands of Dorian warriors entered from the north, forcing the Mycenaean population to **flee** to the coast. As cities burned and fields were left untended, the survivors had no choice but to turn to **piracy**. In some cases, pirates and warriors joined forces to attack the **Egyptian** coast. The Egyptians, horrified by these waves of plunderers and murderers from the Mediterranean, called them in their inscriptions "**the Sea Peoples**."

Many Mycenaean palaces were destroyed, and large parts of Greece were depopulated. Some Greek warlords decided to form an **alliance** to attack the richest and most prosperous city in the region: a legendary enclave called Ilium, but which we know as **Troy**.

The Trojan War was a clear example of the **siege** tactics used by the Sea Peoples.

The story goes that a handful of Greek kings got together and decided to mount a full-scale **attack**. They assembled a phenomenal army of plunderers on a thousand ships with one idea in mind: **to steal**. They intended to take slaves as well, but above all, they were there to steal.

Around the 13th century BC, a surprise attack was launched on the city of **Troy**, and it was besieged. According to mythology, the reason for the attack was that a Greek Queen, **Helen**, had left her husband, the Spartan king Menelaus. She had fled to Troy with her lover, **Paris**, a very handsome Trojan prince. Troy was large and full of riches, but it was protected by **walls** so high and solid that they were said to have been built by the god Poseidon. The Greeks spent a lot of time unsuccessfully attempting to take over the city.

According to the legend, when they were just about to give up, the hero **Ulysses** appeared with a wild idea: to build a gigantic **wooden horse** and leave it there as an offering to the sea god. But it was all a trick, for a battalion of soldiers was hidden inside the horse. The Greeks pretended to leave, but in reality, they hid on a nearby beach. When the Trojans brought the offering into the city, the soldiers jumped out of the horse, killed the guards, and opened the gates to the Greek army. The plan was so crazy that it actually worked: the Greeks robbed, killed, and took slaves for ten days. After that, Troy was **burned** to the ground.

Myth or Reality?

Several centuries later, the story of the Trojan War was the theme of a series of long poems that were compiled into a book called the *Iliad*.

The Greeks believed that the war had really happened, although in time, these poems came to be regarded simply as a **myth**. But a century and a half ago, a Prussian millionaire named **Schliemann** believed that it was real. He set out to excavate a hill on the coast of Turkey that was identical to the place described in the poems, and he unearthed a Mycenaean city. Schliemann was convinced that he had found **the ruins of Troy**. In reality, there were several cities there, all built on top of each other. No one is quite sure which of them is the city depicted in the poems, but today, most experts believe that the Trojan War really **happened**, even if it wasn't quite as it was described in the *Iliad*.

GOSH, THEY COULD'VE PUT THE *DOOR* SOMEWHERE ELSE.

Achilles' Anger

Achilles is one of the main characters in the *Iliad*. In the poem, he is the best soldier among the Greeks, but he is also a thief and a murderer.

At a key point in the story, Achilles gets angry with the general leading the Greek armies and **withdraws** from the fight. The Trojans take the opportunity to attack the Greek camp, and during the battle, Achilles' **best friend** dies at the hands of the Trojan commander **Hector**. Achilles decides to return to the fight to avenge his friend. In the battle, he is consumed by rage and kills a bunch of enemies. When he finds Hector, his friend's murderer, he sets off in relentless pursuit of him, finally managing to finish him off with his **spear**.

THE ARCHAIC PERIOD

8th-5th Centuries BC

The Archaic Period began with the first **Olympic Games** and ended with the war between the Greeks and the Persians.

During this period, the foundations of classical Greek culture were laid: the culture of statues, philosophers, and so on. In the Archaic Period, Greece emerged from the Dark Ages and small villages joined together to form the classic Greek city-states called **poleis**. The poleis soon became too small, and the Greeks began to found new cities called **colonies**. This is also the time when Greek **culture** as we know it took shape. Art, philosophy, and theater all began to develop during this time.

But perhaps the period's most important contribution was in the field of **politics**. Power shifted from the hands of a single person (a **monarchy**) to a handful of selfish, rich people (an **oligarchy**). Tired of obeying them, the citizens of Athens invented a form of government based on the people: **democracy**. The struggle between the democrats and the supporters of rule by the few marked this period as perhaps one of the most interesting in history.

In the early **Archaic Period**, Greece's lands were often attacked by warriors from wilder regions to the north. To deal with them, the villages began to group together and surround their houses with walls, and so the **poleis**, typical in Greek culture, were created.

A polis was an area made up of a city and the surrounding fields, farms, and, if it was by the sea, the harbor. They were usually built around a fortified mound called an **acropolis**, which means "high city."

As they were separated by mountains, each polis was a small, independent state, often at war with other poleis.

Small differences in their customs and points of view prevented them from uniting and forming a large state, even though they spoke the same language and worshipped the same gods.

The problem with the poleis was that they couldn't get very big: if too many people lived there, the farms couldn't produce enough food for everyone. The solution they found was **colonies**: When there were too many people in a polis, part of the population would ship out with their things to found a new city elsewhere.

Sometimes colonies were founded in territories that were already **inhabited** by other peoples. However, the Greeks of the Archaic Period mastered very effective ways of waging **war**, and they usually defeated other less developed peoples easily.

To found a colony, a **leader** was chosen who decided where the future city would be located, which was usually somewhere near the sea. At the beginning, only the men went there in case there was trouble with the locals. After a while, the women and children arrived, bringing with them a **sacred fire**

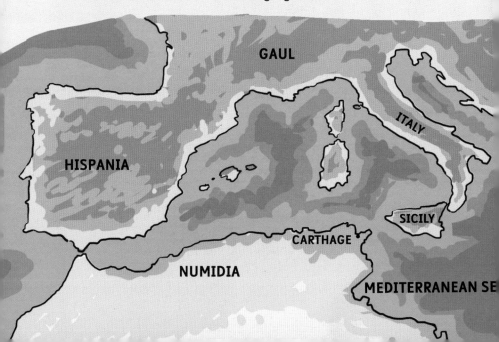

GAUL

ITALY

HISPANIA

SICILY

CARTHAGE

NUMIDIA

MEDITERRANEAN SE

from the original polis. In this new colony, land was divided up in a more rational way.

Some of these colonies became much more important than the original cities. Many **scholars**, philosophers, and artists who later became famous, such as Thales of Miletus, Pythagoras of Croton, and Archimedes of Syracuse, emerged there.

YOU MAY NOT KNOW THAT...

All Greek cities had a place called the **prytaneion**: a group of buildings where the magistrates met and grain was stored. It was dedicated to **Hestia**, the goddess of the hearth, and the sacred fire, which could never be allowed to go out, was kept there. When a new city was founded, a torch lit with the sacred fire of the city of origin was brought to light the fire of the new prytaneion. This act brought the new city under Hestia's protection.

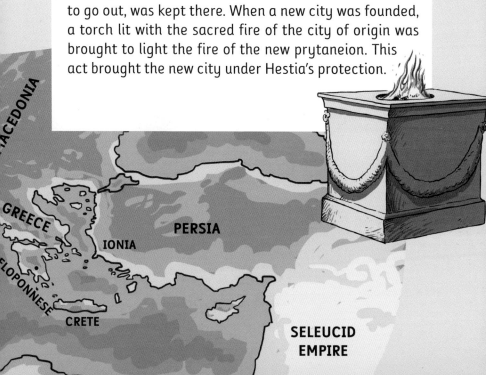

MACEDONIA

GREECE

IONIA

PERSIA

PELOPONNESE

CRETE

SELEUCID
EMPIRE

The Monarchy

At first, the poleis were ruled by a **king**, as in Mycenaean times. One of the king's sons normally **inherited** the title, which was assumed to be of divine origin. It was what is known as a **monarchy**, ruled by one "chosen" person.

The Oligarchy

The kings were gradually replaced by elected rulers called **archons**, although royal power was usually in the hands of a group of rich and powerful men. The rule by the few was called an **oligarchy**, and they called themselves **aristocrats**, meaning "the best."

These aristocrats had great lands cultivated by **slaves**, and they were the only ones who could afford to pay for expensive military equipment: horses, chariots, and armor.

As a result, the aristocrats became increasingly powerful, as they grew **rich** from wars, plundering their rivals' wealth, and enslaving those they captured. Ordinary people, peasants, and craftsmen had no power, and the aristocrats **treated them badly**. The peasants were forced to sell their land to the aristocrats and often had to borrow money from them to feed their families. When they couldn't pay, they ended up becoming their slaves.

Democracy

Democracy was a system of government invented by the Greeks to prevent the rich from abusing the poor. This system originated in **Athens** but spread throughout the entire Greek world.

The idea was that all citizens could **vote** on laws and any of them could be elected to office for a certain period of time. On the whole, the oligarchs **refused** to share power and wished to carry on ruling alone, so those who wanted democracy had to **fight** against them.

People of all classes lived in Greek cities, but they weren't all equal and didn't have the same rights.

The Nobility

These were rich and powerful people that belonged to important families and boasted famous ancestors. As they always married each other, just a few people ended up owning almost all the fertile land, which lots of slaves worked on. The nobles controlled the people with laws and courts, and all ordinary people could do was keep their mouths shut and obey.

The people

In ancient Greece, the ordinary people were **peasants, crafts-men, and workers**. They were citizens of their polis and had certain rights and obligations. Normally, only those who could afford armor and a shield to defend the city were considered citizens.

Democracy in Athens showed that citizens could rebel against the oligarchy and improve their own lives. Many cities threw the nobles out, and the people chose **democracy** as the system of government.

Foreigners, slaves, and women weren't considered citizens of the polis.

Foreigners

Everyone born outside the polis. They were free, but they weren't citizens, so they weren't really taken into account. They couldn't vote or be elected to office.

Slaves

Slaves were neither free nor citizens. They were usually prisoners of war or children of slaves, but you could also end up as a slave if you owed money.

They did the toughest jobs and were held to be rather like talking animals. **Slavery** was normal in all societies in the ancient world, and as a rule, the Greeks treated their slaves better than other peoples of the time.

Women

Women were free, but they weren't citizens. Greek society was as **sexist** as many others of the day, and a women's only role was that of wife and mother. Even so, the Greeks valued **talented** people, and some women excelled in the fields of medicine, science, and art.

During the Archaic Period, the way warfare was conducted **changed**.

The invasions by the Sea Peoples had interrupted the trade in **tin**, a metal that was needed to form **bronze**. Unable to make this essential metal, Mediterranean blacksmiths experimented and discovered a method of extracting **iron** from certain types of rocks that were easy to find.

It was suddenly possible to equip a bunch of people with iron weapons. A warlord named **Pheidon** did this in the city of Argos, and together, they crushed the nobles who fought in chariots Mycenae-style. This proved that citizens' armies were superior to those of the Bronze Age.

The new soldiers were called **hoplites**, which means "armed men." They were each equipped with a long, iron-tipped spear, a helmet, and a circular shield that protected both the soldier carrying it and the one next to him. They also usually wore armor and extra protection on their arms and legs.

During battle, the **hoplites** formed tight rows to better defend themselves. These fighting groups were called **phalanxes**.

Battles were almost always fought in the same way: Two formations of phalanxes, each with several, compact rows, charged forward and clashed against each other, and they all **pushed** each other like crazy. The hoplites behind pushed the ones in front, who tried to thrust their spears into the gaps in the enemy's armor. At some point, one of the two armies would retreat more or less in order. The one that didn't retreat would **win** the battle and erect a kind of monument using the shields that their enemies had left behind.

They also had cavalry, but they were only used to chase retreating soldiers. **Horses** in those days were **smaller** than they are today: They were the size of ponies, and stirrups, which help riders to stay on their horses, hadn't been invented yet. Wars in ancient Greece lasted only a few months, between spring and summer. In late summer, the soldiers had to return to their fields to help with the **harvest**.

According to the ancient Greeks' beliefs, the **gods** weren't everywhere but lived somewhere very specific: on the summit of **Mount Olympus**, the highest mountain in Greece. Neither were they regarded as perfect beings who knew everything. They were powerful, to be sure, but they could be fooled, and they had **faults** like normal people: Hera was jealous, Zeus was unfaithful, Aphrodite was vain, and Ares had an anger management problem.

The Greek gods didn't expect you to behave well, because your **fate** was already written, and there was nothing you could do to avoid what was going to happen to you. What the gods wanted from their worshippers was the occasional animal **sacrifice**.

The most important god was **Zeus**, who had many sons and daughters, all of whom were gods or demigods. When Zeus was angry, he used his lightning to unleash storms or kill those who had disobeyed him. His brother, **Hades**, was the king of the underworld and god of the dead. All mortals ended up there regardless of whether they had behaved well or badly. His other brother was **Poseidon**, the god of the sea.

The goddess of harvests was called **Demeter**. According to the myth, her daughter, **Persephone**, is married to Hades and spends six months of the year with him in the underworld. During those six months, Demeter is sad and nothing grows, but when her daughter comes home to visit her, everything blooms again. This is how they explained the change in the **seasons**.

Other gods were **Dionysus**, the god of wine and amusement, and **Hermes**, the messenger of the gods, who had sandals with wings so that he could run as fast as the wind. **Hephaestus** was a god who was a blacksmith and was married to **Aphrodite**, the goddess of love, although they eventually divorced.

The Greeks had a whole bunch of gods, and it would take several books like this one to name them all.

Poseidon

He was the god of the **sea** and oceans. The Greeks were great seafaring people, so Poseidon was a really important god who sacrifices had to be made to if you wanted to have a good sea voyage.

When Poseidon was angry with mortals, he used his trident to create **storms** that sank ships or caused earthquakes that destroyed cities. He had a lot of children, and he created the first horse by striking a rock with his **trident**.

YOU MAY NOT KNOW THAT...

It is said that Poseidon was sent to protect the city of **Troy** at Zeus' request. With Apollo's help, he built **city walls** so high and strong that no enemy could ever breach them. However, the Trojan king didn't pay the gods the agreed price. Poseidon took this very badly and sent a sea monster called **Ceto** to the city. Years later, the monster would be defeated by **Heracles**.

Athena

As the goddess of strategic **warfare** and **craftsmanship**, the city of **Athens** is named after her. Legend has it that when the Athenians had to choose a god to protect the city, Poseidon and Athena competed for the position. Poseidon stuck his trident into a rock on the Acropolis and made a **spring** of saltwater gush forth as a gift to the city. Athena struck the ground with her spear, and the first **olive tree** that ever existed appeared. A tribunal of gods decided that Athena had won. Olive **oil** became one of the most sought-after products and would be sold all over the Mediterranean.

Heracles

Heracles, whom the Romans called Hercules, was the best known of the Greek mythological **heroes**. He was Zeus' son and had the strength of a god. He was known for undertaking twelve impossible labors.

The first was to kill a lion with his bare hands, and he made himself a cloak with its skin. In another task, he had to kill the **Hydra**, a terrible many-headed monster. Every time Heracles cut off one head, two more grew in its place.

Apollo

Apollo was a very important god: handsome, athletic, and an excellent musician. He was the god of beauty and sport, but also of art, music, archery, the sun, divination, medicine, and **a bunch of other things**.

He was born from a love affair between Zeus and Leto. When Zeus' wife, Hera, found out, she sent Leto to the lands where a **giant snake** called Python lived so the monster could kill her. Apollo got hold of a bow and finished off the horrible snake on Mount Parnassus, at a place called **Delphi**. He then ordered a **temple** to be built there in his honor.

Apollo's Sanctuary at Delphi

Although the Greeks were always fighting each other, there were things that held them together: They spoke the same language and had a common past, such as events like the Trojan War, when all Greeks formed a single army. There was also the fact that they all worshipped the same gods, and that is why there were **sanctuaries**, which, in a way, belonged to all Greeks. One of the most important was Apollo's sanctuary at Delphi.

The sanctuary was a **sacred precinct** protected by walls that enclosed several temples surrounded by gardens with fountains, statues, and a theater.

Visitors to Delphi had to climb up a slope surrounded by miniature temples where offerings to the gods were kept. At the top was the impressive Temple of Apollo. There was always a long line to get in because there was something special inside the temple: the **Oracle of Delphi**.

The Oracle of Delphi

The Oracle was the system by which people asked the priestess, whose nickname was **Pythia** (source of the word "pythoness," meaning a woman who practices divination), about Apollo's will. When the priests guarding the temple let them in, visitors could ask about whom they should marry, whether they should go on a journey, or anything else. Cities even sent **delegations** to ask about such important matters as going to war or founding a new colony.

Once a questioner entered the sacred precinct, he had to offer Apollo a honey **cake** and sacrifice a **goat**. Before the animal was killed, sacred water was poured over it. If the goat trembled, it meant that Apollo would come to talk.

Those who were able to enter the temple had to ask a question. Pythia would give an **ambiguous answer** which could be understood in various ways. The priests were in charge of **interpreting** her words and communicating them to the person concerned. Some say that Pythia sat on a chair over a crack in the ground which gave off toxic fumes that made her **hallucinate**.

The **prophecies** were expressed in very vague words. That way, whatever happened, the priests could always say that the prophecy had been misinterpreted.

Croesus and the Persians

A very well-known case was that of **Croesus**, the last king of **Lydia**, in the 6th century BC. Croesus was considered the richest man in the world, but this wasn't enough for him, and he decided to expand his kingdom by invading lands belonging to the king of **Persia**. To be on the safe side, he asked the Oracle if it would be a good idea for him to go to war. Pythia told him that, if he did, a great empire would be destroyed. Croesus attacked the Persians, but he was defeated, and the Persian army stormed the palace and captured him.

Pythia had been **right** again. By attacking the Persians, Croesus had destroyed a great empire: **his own**.

In the Archaic Period, Greek society underwent major **changes**. The best lands ended up in the hands of a few, and more and more citizens wound up as slaves to the rich. But, in order to **defend** the city, you needed a whole bunch of free men with enough money to pay for a shield, armor, and helmet.

To avoid revolutions, many cities ceded broad powers to **lawgivers**, who created laws to make societies a little fairer.

Solon the lawgiver (638-558 BC)

Solon the lawgiver was elected to bring order to Athens and avoid a civil war between the nobles and the people. Until he showed up, a few noble families shared the power, made the laws, and were the judges.

Solon **banned** the enslaving of peasants and tried to **share out** the best land, which was held by the nobles, among everyone. He extended the opportunity to hold public office to more people—but only the richest. Solon's reforms were important, but the **poorest** people still had a hard time and demanded more basic changes which wouldn't come until democracy was born.

Spartan Society

In the south of Greece lies the **Peloponnese** peninsula. One of its regions, Laconia, was conquered by **Dorian tribes** during the Dark Ages, and the famous city of **Sparta** was founded there. The Dorians demanded that the local population surrender and become their servants. Those who submitted, who were called **Perioeci**, became craftsmen and traders, but they weren't considered citizens and had no rights. Those who refused to submit willingly were subjected to the most brutal slavery. Nicknamed **helots**, their lot was pretty appalling because the Spartans were bullies.

Lycurgus (some time between the 9th and 7th centuries BC)

Lycurgus was a lawgiver in Sparta, although no one really knows whether he actually existed. He is said to have written the laws by which Sparta governed itself in the years that followed. They were based on the distribution of wealth among citizens, compulsory military service, and state education of young people.

When he had finished writing the laws, he went on a journey, but first he made the Spartans promise to **obey** the laws until he returned. According to legend, as soon as he left the city, he committed **suicide** so that his laws would be respected forever.

LYCURGUS

The *Agoge* or Spartan Education

Spartan **babies** were examined by the priests at birth. If they were sickly or had any defects, they were sent rolling down a hill. Only those who showed initiative and clung to a branch were saved.

Spartan boys were raised at home until they were **seven**. At that age, they were sent to the barracks and trained as **soldiers**.

In the barracks, they were beaten for any reason. They went **barefoot** and wore summer clothes all year round, so that they would get used to having a hard time. The children received very little food, so they were forced to sneak out and steal from nearby farms. If they were caught stealing, they were beaten with sticks—not for the stealing, but for getting caught.

The young men had to pass a final **test** at the age of **eighteen** before being accepted as citizens: to challenge a young, strong slave as a potential helot leader and kill him with their bare hands.

This brutal educational system wasn't aimed at training better soldiers, but at making them insensitive and **obedient**. And it worked. While elsewhere in Greece there were revolutions, tyrannies, and democratic regimes, Spartan society remained true to its traditions for much longer.

Once accepted as **citizens**, Spartans were allocated plots of land and their own slaves, who would cultivate those plots. After all, the Spartans weren't farmers or craftsmen; their only skill was soldiering. They weren't even allowed to live at home but had to sleep in the barracks. If they wanted to see their **wives**, they had to sneak out at night and be back before daylight. This meant that Spartan women enjoyed a little more **independence** than other Greek women, because they were in charge of their farms' affairs while their husbands were away training or killing people.

During the Archaic Period, the Greek poleis were in constant **turmoil**. On one side were the rich, who were always fighting among themselves for more money and power. On the other side were the ordinary people, who were peasants, craftsmen, and workers who counted for nothing.

In these circumstances, men often emerged who gained power by **force** and held on to it by protecting the poor from the abuses of the rich. They were called **tyrants**.

Perhaps surprisingly, the poleis **improved** and grew richer under tyrannies because the tyrants tried to keep the people **happy** for fear that they would rebel. They often used the city's resources to build temples, harbors, and waterways, which provided employment for local workers and craftsmen.

The tyrants rose to power through their exploits and personal charisma. If they survived long enough, they tried to have their **heirs** carry on their work, but this hardly ever worked out well. The rich used to take advantage of the slightest opportunity to assassinate or expel new tyrants and re-impose the oligarchy.

Pittacus of Mytilene (640-568 BC)

One very famous tyrant was Pittacus, a highly **intelligent** man who ruled the polis of Mytilene. When his city went to **war** against the Athenians, he was elected general and marched to the battlefield at the head of his troops. There he encountered **Phrynon**, the Athenian general, the winner of the Olympic Games, and a man known throughout Greece for his strength and courage.

As the two sides were very evenly matched, Pittacus proposed **combat** between just the two of them, which would decide the outcome of the battle. Phrynon agreed, but during the fight, Pittacus trapped Phrynon in a net and killed him in front of everyone. The Athenians retreated without a fight.

In gratitude for saving the lives of so many soldiers, the city of Mytilene offered him the office of tyrant. After ten years of rule, Pittacus resigned and devoted himself to teaching **philosophy**. He is held to be the best ruler Mytilene ever had.

The Sword of Damocles

In the 4th century BC, a tyrant named **Dionysius I** ruled the city of **Syracuse**. A member of his private council, **Damocles**, was always telling Dionysius how lucky he was. Dionysius suggested that Damocles should be tyrant for a day.

The next day, Damocles was treated like a king. Everyone gathered around him as he took the place of honor at the table. Suddenly, he noticed that everyone was gazing at him in fear: above his head, a huge **sword** hung from the ceiling, tied with a single horsehair. Damocles couldn't enjoy the food, the wine, or the court's adulation. By setting things up this way, Dionysus was trying to make him understand that the life of a tyrant could be full of pleasures and honors but also **dangers**, because the rich were always trying to kill them in order to regain power.

Pisistratus (607-527 BC)

The first tyrant of Athens was named **Pisistratus**. When he was appointed admiral of the fleet, he conquered several ports and re-established the trade routes that supplied the city with food.

The famine ended, merchants and craftsmen were making money, and everyone saw Pisistratus as the man who had brought **prosperity** to Athens. At that time, the city oligarchs were divided into two **camps** that were always quarreling: the landowners and the merchants. Pisistratus created a **third** party: one for the poor, workers, and peasants. The people adored him because he promised to distribute land and aid, but the rich hated him.

One fine day, he showed up in the square wounded and covered in blood, saying that his enemies had tried to kill him. The citizens gave him a **guard** of fifty men for his protection. It was a trick: He had wounded himself to get these soldiers, which he used to seize the acropolis and proclaim himself tyrant.

It didn't last long. As soon as he began to pass laws protecting the peasants, his political enemies put aside their differences and **joined together** to expel him from the city. Pisistratus' first tyranny only lasted **six months**.

A year later, he reappeared. This time, he made a grand entrance: He arrived in Athens in a chariot that appeared to be driven by **Athena** herself, the goddess of the city. People came out into the streets to see him pass by, and the news spread everywhere: Pisistratus, defender of the poor, had returned to the city. The supposed goddess was actually a girl from the mountains **dressed up**. Even his enemies believed that the gods were on his side.

Pisistratus' Triumph

Pisistratus' political enemies once again united to **expel** him from the city and seize his property.

In exile, Pisistratus went into **business** and became a wealthy man. He earned enough money to finance an army, and aided by his two sons, he returned to Athens to seize power by force. He proclaimed himself tyrant for the **third** time. He confiscated his enemies' huge **estates**, divided them into smaller plots, and gave them back to the peasants who had been left landless. He also provided work for laborers and craftsmen by ordering the construction of temples, theaters, and an aqueduct. He ruled Athens until his death in 527 BC.

Pisistratus' Sons

The whole city attended Pisistratus' **burial**, and it was decided that his two sons, **Hippias and Hipparchus**, would inherit the government. Pisistratus' sons were young and rich. They

had also proved themselves to be brave, and people loved them as much as their father. They knew how to rule wisely, as their father had taught them.

Hipparchus liked a boy named **Harmodius**, but Harmodius already had a boyfriend named **Aristogeiton**. Together, they decided to kill Hipparchus. They intended to kill Hippias as well to prevent him from taking revenge, but they didn't succeed because he had a bodyguard. Both were put to death for the murder of Hipparchus.

Hippias

Hippias was left to rule alone, but his brother's murder made him paranoid. His character changed, and he began to abuse his power until he became a **tyrant** in the modern sense of the term.

His enemies **bribed** the priests of the Oracle of Delphi to persuade the **Spartans** to intervene and expel Hippias from Athens. Hippias' defeated supporters took refuge in the Acropolis.

When the Spartans captured his sons, Hippias promised to leave if they weren't harmed. In 510 BC, he left for Persia, where he managed to gain the confidence of King **Darius I**.

After the expulsion of Hippias, a unique event took place in Athens: the creation of the first-known democracy in human history. Athenian democracy was a **direct democracy**: the citizens met once a week and participated in political decisions by voting, for example, on whether to go to war or sign peace treaties, or to decide how to spend money from taxes.

The meeting of all the citizens, where everyone could speak and vote, was called an **assembly**.

In the 5th century BC, **Pericles**, a general, decided that magistrates should receive payment, because he considered them to be serving the city. Thanks to this, people who didn't have the time or money to be present were included in Athens' political life.

Citizens were elected to public office in two different ways:

• **By drawing lots**. This was the most common method of appointing public officials, as it was considered the most democratic possible: all citizens had to govern and be governed in turn. So, no type of advantage or merit was taken into account when electing them.

• **By voting**. Around a hundred officials were elected by the assembly. They had specific tasks, such as market inspectors or judges, who were elected only once in a lifetime. They were vetted before and after taking office to prevent corruption.

Modern democracies differ from ancient Greek democracy in that, nowadays, citizens only have the right to elect officials who represent them and vote on laws on their behalf.

The Sanctuary of Zeus in Olympia

In southern Greece, on the **Peloponnese** peninsula, one of the ancient world's greatest religious and sporting centers was built: the **Sanctuary of Olympia**.

For centuries, religious rituals and sporting competitions involving citizens from all the Greek poleis were held at Olympia every four years. These were the **Olympic Games**.

During the month before the Games were held, messengers would announce a sacred **truce** throughout Greece: battles and wars were stopped so that athletes and spectators could go to Olympia safely.

The **competitions** consisted of long jump, discus and javelin throwing, chariot races, fighting, and footraces, some in full armor.

There were also music, art, and poetry competitions. The winners received no money, only a **wreath** of olive branches. However, when they returned to their hometowns, they were **honored** with poems, songs, and sometimes even statues.

Sexist Games

Women were forbidden to attend or participate in the Olympic Games. But in the 5th century BC, a woman called Pherenice of Rhodes, nicknamed **Kallipateira**, mother of the famous champion Peisirodos, wasn't willing to miss her son's triumph. She dressed as a coach and managed to sneak into the stadium, pretending to be a man. When her son won his fight, she jumped over the fence to congratulate him, but her **robe** got caught; she was left standing naked in front of everyone.

According to Olympic rules, women who broke the law were thrown off Mount Typaion. But since Kallipateira was the daughter, sister, and mother of famous Olympic champions, the judges decided to spare her thanks to her family's influence. To prevent a repetition of this, a new **rule** was enacted requiring coaches and athletes to be **naked** at all times to make sure that they were men.

The most important contests in the Games were the **fights**. There were three types of fighting: **wrestling**, in which blows weren't allowed; **boxing**, in which only punches were allowed; and **pankration**, which was a mixture of the two and in which everything was allowed except biting and gouging out your opponent's eyes.

Athletes such as **Dioxippus of Athens** became famous in pankration. Everyone who had fought him had been badly wounded. On one occasion, in 336 BC, he won without fighting even once because all the fighters withdrew one after the other so that they wouldn't have to face him. Another famous wrestler was **Sostratus**, who was known as "**Fingertips**" because he would immobilize his opponent as soon as he could and break his fingers until he surrendered.

YOU MAY NOT KNOW THAT...

Pankration was such a violent sport that the fighters sometimes **died**. However, there were cases in which one of them was declared the winner even after his death. This was the case with a competitor called **Arrhichion** in 564 BC: During the fight, Arrhichion was being strangled by the other fighter. With his last breath, he dislocated the ankle of his opponent, who surrendered because of the pain. When the judges went to proclaim Arrhichion the winner, they found him dead.

Another curious case was the fight between **Creugas and Damoxenos** in 400 BC. The contest was so close that the judges decided that they had to punch each other until one of the two either fell or surrendered. Damoxenos overstepped the mark and killed Creugas, but the judges decided to award the victory to Creugas because they considered Damoxenos' final blow to have been illegal.

THE CLASSICAL PERIOD

5th-4th Centuries BC

The Classical Period is the era in Greek history between the Ionian Revolt and the reign of Alexander the Great.

This period began with the wars against Persia and continued with the establishment of democracy in Athens and the Golden Age of Greek art and culture, which coincided with the rule of the most brilliant politician of his day: **Pericles**. This was the historical period in which the power of the Greek poleis and the cultural manifestations that developed in them reached their peak.

Greek **art**, especially sculpture, reached levels of perfection in the Classical Period that made it a model for the Roman Empire, Renaissance Europe, and neoclassical artistic movements.

At the beginning of the 5th century BC, **Athens** was becoming the richest and most important city in Greece. The experiment with a government in which all citizens participated was proving a great success, and democratic ideas were beginning to spread throughout the Greek world.

However, on the other side of the sea, a superpower was threatening Greece's prosperity. It was the **Persian Empire**, which had conquered the entire Middle East and Egypt and subdued northern Greece. Along the way, some Greek **colonies** had been forced to submit to the Persian king, give up their independence, and pay huge taxes.

At this point, the cities in the Greek region of **Ionia** decided to revolt against Persia and ask for help from European Greece. Only Athens and Eretria sent help to the Ionians. Twenty warships and two thousand soldiers left Athens to assist the rebel cities.

The Greeks attacked the center of Persian power in the region, the wealthy city of **Sardis**. However, the Persians mobilized their troops, and within weeks they appeared with a gigantic army followed by a fleet of hundreds of warships, ready to retake Sardis. Faced with this show of force, the rebel cities surrendered one after the other. The revolt quickly **failed**.

But in his palace at Susa, the Persian king Darius I was plotting his **revenge** against the insignificant Greek cities that had dared defy him. One of his advisors was **Hippias**, the former tyrant of Athens, who proposed landing on the beach at **Marathon**, some twenty-six miles from Athens. Hippias had a large following in the city and was convinced that as soon as they heard that he had returned, they would open the gates of the city, and he would be proclaimed tyrant.

The following summer, the Persian fleet attacked the Greek islands that had aided the rebels, and shortly afterward, in 490 BC, the army landed on the plain of Marathon.

When they saw what was coming, the Athenians sent a professional runner named **Pheidippides** to Sparta to ask for help against the Persians.

The Persian king had nothing against Sparta; besides, the Spartans were celebrating a religious festival and weren't planning on going anywhere for a few days. The Athenian army arrived at Marathon and took up positions in the **hills**, from where they could see the beach where the enemy was located. There were six Persians to every Athenian, and they had a fearsome cavalry, but the Athenians had the advantage of height. Moreover, their troops were better trained, better equipped, and better motivated than the Persian recruits, so the two armies held their positions for five days without either of them deciding to attack.

The Athenians knew that time was on their side; the Spartan army would show up in a few days, and everyone knew what they were like. However, there were many in Athens who thought it better to surrender to the Persians and restore Hippias as tyrant.

On the fifth day, the Persians began to mobilize. From high in the hills, the Athenian general **Miltiades** watched the Persians beginning to load their troops onto the ships, starting with the horses. Miltiades suspected that the Persians were planning to land in Athens itself, taking advantage of the fact that all the Athenian soldiers were at Marathon. When half of the Persian army had boarded, Miltiades ordered his men to get into formation and charge the enemy. The most important **battle** in Greek history was about to begin.

The Battle of Marathon

At Miltiades' order, **ten thousand Athenians** set off running down the hill, laden with their heavy military equipment. The Persians didn't realize what was happening until it was too late. They tried to close ranks and stop the Greeks with a volley of arrows, but because they were running so fast, the arrows flew over their heads.

From a very young age, the Athenians were used to competing in a type of **race** in which they had to run wearing armor and carrying a shield, so they had no trouble reaching the Persian ranks together. It is said that the **clash** of the ten thousand shields against the Persian weapons could be heard for miles around.

The Persians were virtually raw recruits. They wore no armor, and their shields were made of wood. The Athenians wore helmets, shields, and iron armor, so they swept them from the battlefield. The Persians broke ranks and tried to **flee** to the ships, while the Athenians pursued them and slaughtered them by the thousand.

It was a great victory for the Greeks, but there was a problem: many Persians had managed to embark and were already sailing at full speed for unprotected **Athens**. Miltiades knew that Athens housed many supporters of Hippias, the son of the tyrant Pisistratus, who wanted to open the city gates to the invaders. To prevent this, Miltiades once again turned to the runner **Pheidippides**: This time, he sent him to Athens to report the victory so that the Athenians wouldn't be tempted to surrender.

YOU MAY NOT KNOW THAT...

Pheidippides ran the **twenty-six miles** from Marathon to Athens, carrying all his military equipment so the Athenians wouldn't think that he'd deserted.

When he reached Athens' main square and people gathered around him to find out what had happened, Pheidippides shouted "*Nike!*" (which means "Victory!") and dropped dead on the spot. No one knows whether it was heat stroke or wounds sustained in the battle that killed him.

The Athenians barricaded themselves in the city, and when the Persians arrived, they found that no one would open the gates, so they turned back and went home.

Today, the twenty-six-mile race is called a **marathon** in honor of Pheidippides' sacrifice.

King Darius died shortly after the Battle of Marathon, and his son **Xerxes** wanted to attack Greece again. Fortunately for the Greeks, Xerxes was kept busy for several years putting down a rebellion in Egypt.

Meanwhile, in Athens, the **democratic revolution** was still going on: The citizens' assembly had become the highest authority in the city. Everyone was aware of the threat of a Persian invasion, so they decided to consult the Oracle of Delphi, who prophesied that Athens would be razed to the ground and "only the wooden walls would remain unconquered." The Athenians wondered which wooden walls the **prophecy** referred to. Some believed that they should build a wooden wall around the **Acropolis** and hold out there, even if the rest of the polis was destroyed.

Themistocles, a leading politician of the day, didn't believe this interpretation: He was convinced that Athens should have a fleet and that "wooden walls" was a way of referring to **warships**.

A new type of ship was coming into use at the time. These ships were called **triremes**, because they had three tiers of rowers. Triremes were faster and easier to maneuver than the older ships, but they were very **expensive** to build.

However, luck seemed to be with the Athenians. Large **silver mines** had been discovered to the south of the city, and meanwhile, Xerxes was still stuck in Egypt. Suddenly, the Athenians were rich. But what were they going to do with the money? Some suggested sharing it out, but Themistocles didn't believe that a handful of coins in the citizens' pockets would be any use if they were attacked. When he was put in charge of the city's defenses, he used the money to build a **fleet of triremes** with which Athens could defend its freedom and independence at sea.

YOU MAY NOT KNOW THAT...

The triremes' main weapon was the **ram**, a piece of metal used, as its name indicates, to ram and sink enemy ships. Another **tactic** at which Greek sailors excelled was to get alongside an enemy ship and turn suddenly. In this way, they broke the oars on one side of the ship, so it would then be left going round in circles and very vulnerable to attack.

THE SECOND GRECO-PERSIAN WAR

The Battle of Thermopylae

The Second Greco-Persian War lasted from 480 to 478 BC. While the Athenians were building their fleet, Xerxes had put down the rebellion in Egypt and was ready to **attack**. The powerful Persian army, advancing from the north, conquered Macedonia and northern Greece. Compared to the Persian army, the one assembled by the Greeks was very small. Themistocles therefore proposed to face the Persians in the **Thermopylae**, a gorge with high cliffs on one side and a precipice on the other. The Persians could only send in a small group of soldiers at a time there, and their far greater numbers would be of no use to them.

The plan worked, and the Greeks held the Persians for **a week**. However, a local Greek named **Ephialtes** betrayed his own people and showed the Persians a mountain road by which they could surround the Greeks, who had to retreat. They used their fleet to evacuate the city, and as they left their home, they saw the Persians entering Athens and **setting fire** to the city.

The 300

When they learned that they were about to be surrounded, most of the Greek soldiers withdrew.

However, the Spartan king **Leonidas** wouldn't hear of it. For one thing, the Spartans had a reputation for never **surrendering**. Besides, someone had to protect the retreat.

Leonidas was over sixty years old, making him a very old man for the times, and he knew that this would be his **last** battle. He didn't want to die in bed, so he was determined to fight to the end and be remembered as a hero.

All the Spartans and a thousand Greeks from other cities **died** in that last battle. At the site, a **monument** was erected with the inscription: "Go tell the Spartans, stranger passing by, that here, obedient to their laws, we lie."

The Battle of Salamis

After the defeat at Thermopylae, the people of Athens used their new fleet to escape to the island of **Salamis**.

Many Athenians believed that it was best to leave Greece and found a new city elsewhere. Themistocles disagreed and came up with an idea: He sent a message to Xerxes **pretending to betray** the Greeks. The message said that the entire Greek fleet was at Salamis and that, if he attacked there with all his might, he would win a great victory because the Greeks wouldn't be able to escape. Xerxes believed it and sent all his ships to the island.

His plan **worked** perfectly. The Greek sailors, who were trapped, had no choice but to fight—whether they wanted to or not. The Battle of Salamis would be remembered as one of the greatest sea conflicts of all time.

The Persian fleet was significantly larger than the Greek fleet, but the **location** Themistocles had chosen worked in the Greeks' favor.

In such a **narrow** place, the Persian ships got in each other's way and couldn't maneuver properly. The Greek fleet attacked them as they tried to organize themselves, sinking and boarding ships. Many Persian ships tried to withdraw, but they collided with each other and ended up crashing against the rocks.

The final outcome was a great **victory** for the Greeks and a monumental defeat for the Persians. Without a fleet to bring their army supplies, the invasion of Greece was doomed to fail. A year later, a combined Greek army attacked the Persians at **Plataea** and defeated them. The Persians withdrew and never again attempted to conquer Greece.

Artemisia of Caria (5th century BC) was the first woman to command a war **fleet**. Since she had proved her ability as a strategist in several battles, **Xerxes** gave her command of five Persian triremes and included her in his private council. Before the battle of Salamis, Xerxes assembled his captains to show them the plan of attack. All the admirals agreed on attacking the Greeks at **Salamis** except for Artemisia, who warned that the site of the battle favored the enemy. However, Xerxes ignored her.

When the battle began, Artemisia was surrounded by Greek ships. She decided to get out before she was captured, but a Persian trireme was blocking her way, so she rammed it to get through. The Greeks, upon seeing that she was destroying an enemy ship, thought her ship was one of theirs and let her though.

Artemisia' ship was one of the few to **escape** disaster. If Xerxes had listened to her, the battle might have ended very differently.

The Oarsmen

If the Greek fleet was superior to the Persian, it wasn't because of the quality of the ships, for the Persian and Greek triremes were identical. The difference was the oarsmen: The Greek oarsmen were too poor to afford armor and fight as hoplites, but they were free men who fought to prevent their city from being razed to the ground and their wives and children from being enslaved by the Persians. The oarsmen of the Persian fleet, on the other hand, were **slaves**. Whether they won or lost, they would remain slaves, so they didn't row with much enthusiasm. Most came from the inland Persian deserts and couldn't swim, so many **drowned** when their boats went down.

After the battle, the Athenians realized the oarsmen's importance and decided to grant them the same privileges as the hoplites. Thus, the last obstacle to participating in democracy, namely money, had been removed forever.

ANOTHER *BEE'S* GOTTEN INTO THE TRIREME!

PERICLES

Not long after the Persians were defeated, the democrat leader, **Pericles**, (495-429 BC) won the elections. Pericles tried to involve all Athenian citizens in the government. It was he who decided to pay a **salary** in return for services to the state and that some offices should be filled by drawing lots from among all Athenian citizens.

At that time, Greek cities had formed an alliance to defend themselves against Persian aggression. It was called the **Delian League**. All cities had to contribute warships to a fleet led by the Athenians, but some cities preferred to give money instead of ships. Pericles used the money to rebuild the Acropolis of Athens, which the Persians had razed to the ground during the war. There he decided to erect a splendid temple that would house a huge statue of Athena: the **Parthenon**. Its construction, which lasted from 447 to 432 BC, gave work to the poorest citizens and made Athens both the most magnificent city of its time and an important center for art and literature.

Athena Parthenos

Inside the temple stood a spectacular **statue** of Athena, made of wood and covered with gold plate and ivory. In her hand, she held a girl with wings and a laurel wreath, the symbol of victory. Scenes from the battle against the Persians were painted on the inside of her shield. It had been made by the man who was in charge of the construction of the building, a friend of Pericles called **Phidias**.

Rumor had it that he had portrayed himself in some of the scenes, which was considered in bad taste at the time.

Phidias' workshop was also responsible for the **reliefs** that decorated the façade of the building. Because of these works, Phidias was considered the ancient world's greatest sculptor.

Outside the temple, Phidias created another huge statue, this time in bronze, called the *Lemnian Athena*. When ships arrived in Athens, the first thing the sailors saw was the sun reflected on the tip of Athena's spear.

Pericles had many **enemies**: all the rich men who had ruled the city for years. In their view, it was Pericles' fault that the most important offices were now held by ordinary citizens instead of them. However, attacking Pericles was difficult because he was too popular, so they went after Phidias instead, accusing him of having kept some of the **gold** that covered the statue of Athena. He was found guilty and sent to prison, where he died in 432 BC.

YOU MAY NOT KNOW THAT...

After he created the magnificent *Athena Parthenos*, the Olympia council commissioned Phidias to create a sculpture of Zeus. Also made of gold and ivory, the Greeks considered this statue to be one of the Seven Wonders of the Ancient World.

For centuries, the Greeks made **statues** to honor the gods and important people. These sculptures were similar to those made by other peoples, such as the Egyptians: the bodies appeared **stiff** and expressionless, they always faced forward, and each wore a slightly forced smile. In the Classical Period, however, everything suddenly changed: Within a few years, Greek sculptors were striving for perfection, **realism**, and the ideal of beauty.

Greek statues were usually made of **bronze** and painted in bright, realistic **colors**. Unfortunately, bronze is very expensive; sometime later, the statues were **melted down** for the metal and were lost forever.

COME ON MAN. JUST *THROW* IT.

Only a few pieces that were forgotten or left behind by looters have come down to us.

But when the **Romans** conquered Greece, Greek sculpture came back into fashion. All Romans with a little money wanted Greek statues to decorate their gardens, and they commissioned copies of the most famous ones, also in full color but in a cheaper material: **marble**. Roman workshops produced hundreds of copies which were scattered throughout the entire Empire. When they were overrun by the barbarians, the statues were buried in the rubble of villas and palaces. Over time, some of them showed up here and there. After centuries under the earth, they had **lost all their color**.

Sculptors who tried to imitate the Greek style in later centuries used **white marble** and left the statues unpainted.

Among the typical works in Greek culture were **temples** with gabled roofs supported by **columns**. Temples were places that served to protect the statues of the gods to which they were dedicated. They were usually built of limestone and wood, and they usually weren't very large because the ceremonies and rituals took place outside. Like the statues, Greek temples were painted in bright **colors** and decorated with **reliefs**, which were also painted.

From ancient times, the Greeks distinguished three **orders**—that is, three ways of building temples—which were based on the different shapes of their columns. The oldest order was called **Doric**: traditional in Sparta and the Peloponnese in general, it was usually used for male gods such as Zeus and Poseidon. The **Ionic** style was typical of the region of Athens and Ionia, which is the part of Asia Minor that is closest to Greece. You will recognize it easily by the snail-shaped decorations, called volutes, on the capitals (the top of the columns). The third style has a legend all of its own. It is said that, one day, a girl left a basket behind near a quarry in Corinth. An acanthus plant grew around the basket, the stonemasons liked it, and they began to sculpt capitals in that shape. Thus, the **Corinthian** style, typical of the architecture of the Hellenistic and Roman period, was born.

DORIC

IONIC

CORINTHIAN

The Temple of Artemis at Ephesus

The largest temple ever built was at Ephesus, in modern-day **Turkey**. It was dedicated to Artemis, goddess of hunting and fertility. The temple was built in the **Ionic** style using white marble. The bases of the columns were decorated with painted **reliefs**, and the interior contained sculptures by the greatest masters of ancient times. The temple was so impressive that the Greeks of the Hellenistic period considered it one of the Seven Wonders of the Ancient World.

On 21 July 356 BC, the day that Alexander the Great was born, a madman set **fire** to the temple from inside. The fire spread rapidly, and the building was engulfed in flames. When he was caught, the man said he had done it to become **famous** and make his name known to the world. The Ephesians forbade his name to be recalled on pain of death, but it has come down to us. His name was **Herostratus**.

Greek theater grew out of **poems** performed by an actor during festivals in honor of **Dionysus**, the god of wine and amusement. Eventually, things got more complicated: More actors were included, a chorus of singers and dancers were added, and the stories became more complex. At first, the theater only dealt with **mythological** themes, but it soon began to cover **current affairs**, such as the war against Persia.

The actors wore **distinctive** masks, and the plays had musical accompaniments. A special **crane-like** machine was used for some scenes involving the gods, and the actor playing whichever god seemed to descend from the sky to play his part.

At first, the theaters were built of **wood**, but after a disastrous fire in the Athens theater, they began to be made of **stone**. The first permanent theater in Athens was built by **Pisistratus**.

Theaters were divided into three parts: There was the **stage**, a raised platform for the actors which was usually decorated with columns and painted backdrops; in front of the stage was an area called the **orchestra**, where the chorus danced and sang at certain points in the performance; and finally, the audience sat on seats arranged in a **semicircle**, with a place of honor in the front rows for important people.

Some theaters were so well-built that they are still in use today.

The most famous **athlete** of the ancient world lived during the Classical Period. His name was **Milo of Croton**, which was a Greek colony in Italy, and he became famous by winning all the **pankration** competitions for twenty-four years in a row.

He failed the qualifying rounds for his first fight, and the other fighters mocked him because he was very thin. That was when he invented what we now call **progressive training**: He bought a newborn **calf** and would walk around Croton carrying it on his shoulders every day. As time went on, Milo grew stronger, but the calf also grew, so the weight Milo was carrying became heavier and heavier.

Before his first fight, he carried the calf around the stadium at Olympia, sacrificed it, offered the skin and bones to the gods, and ate the rest. He won in many competitions: the Olympic Games, the Pythian Games held at Delphi, the Isthmian Games at Corinth, and the Nemean Games. He **retired** from professional fighting in his forties.

At that time, Croton was also home to a very famous scholar called **Pythagoras**. One day, when Pythagoras was teaching mathematics, the school **roof** collapsed. Milo, who was there, held up the roof on his shoulders until the teacher and all his pupils could get out safely. The athlete ended up marrying Pythagoras' daughter, **Myia**.

Near Croton was a city called **Sybaris**. The **Sybarites** were known for their luxurious and sophisticated way of life. There was even said to be a man who slept on rose petals but complained that his bed was uncomfortable because one of the petals was bent. That is why the word "sybarite" is used today to refer to someone who loves expensive and refined pleasures, especially where food is concerned.

The Sybarites were very fond of **parades**. They are said to have taught their horses to march in time to the music. When Croton declared war on them in 510 BC, Pythagoras came up with a brilliant plan to defeat the Sybarites using their own horses. In addition to soldiers, Croton brought with them a lot of musicians who began to play. The Sybarites' horses thought they were in a parade, and instead of charging the enemy, they began to dance. Thus, the Sybarite soldiers couldn't even defend themselves.

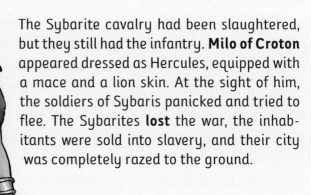

The Sybarite cavalry had been slaughtered, but they still had the infantry. **Milo of Croton** appeared dressed as Hercules, equipped with a mace and a lion skin. At the sight of him, the soldiers of Sybaris panicked and tried to flee. The Sybarites **lost** the war, the inhabitants were sold into slavery, and their city was completely razed to the ground.

YOU MAY NOT KNOW THAT...

The destruction of Sybaris was an exception, being one of the few cases in which one Greek city completely destroyed another. The Crotonians even diverted the course of the River Crati so that it **flooded** the area where the city had been.

Years later, some visitors wanted to see the ruins. However, Sybaris had been so entirely destroyed that no one knew where to find the legendary city from whose springs, the legends said, wine had once flowed.

The Strange Death of Milo of Croton

When Milo was an old man, he was walking through a forest, and he came across a **tree** that had a wedge jammed into a crevice that had been left by woodcutters.

Milo wanted to split the tree with his owns hands to prove to himself that he was still as strong as when he was young. However, as soon as he removed the wedge, the two parts of the trunk came together and **trapped** his hands. He tried to get free for several hours, but he only succeeded in tiring himself out.

When night fell, a pack of **wolves** appeared in the forest looking for something to eat. When they saw Milo helpless, they didn't think twice and devoured him on the spot.

Corinth

The Second Greco-Persian War was followed by **fifty years of peace**, during which Athens became the most powerful city in Greece. With its fleet and Delian League allies, Athens was able to control trade in that part of the Mediterranean. But in the Peloponnesian city of **Corinth**, no one was happy for the Athenians.

Corinth had been the richest city before the Greco-Persian Wars, and its fleet was the most powerful. As Athens grew larger, Corinth grew smaller. In the end, the two cities went to war over control of the island of **Korkyra**, now called Corfu. However, the Corinthians had an alliance with **Sparta**, which declared war on Athens.

The Long Walls

Everyone knew that Sparta had the best army in Greece. The Spartans were psychopaths who would rather die than sur-render, and Pericles knew that trying to defeat them in open battle was suicide, so he opted for another strategy.

Shortly before this, Athens had completed the construc-tion of what were called the **Long Walls**. These were an exten-sion of the city walls, which were joined to those protecting the harbor, creating a **corridor** through which supplies could be transported safely from the harbor to the city.

The idea was that, as soon as the Spartans arrived, all the region's inhabitants would **take refuge** inside the walls with their provisions and their animals. The Spartans would be unable to fight a decisive battle and would end up withdrawing after a few days. For their part, the Athenians could use the fleet to bring supplies to the city and attack the coastal cities that were allied with Sparta.

The plan worked perfectly, and after burning the farms and fields, the Spartans **withdrew** in time for the harvest.

The Plague of Athens

Pericles had no way of knowing that his strategy, ingenious as it seemed, would mean the **end** of Athens' dominance forever.

In the following year, 430 BC, ships carrying wheat from Egypt to Athens brought the **plague**, an infectious disease that spread quickly within Athens' overcrowded walls. The disease killed one in three Athenians, weakening their army and navy. Pericles himself died of the plague alongside his sons. When the Spartans returned that summer and found out what was happening, they withdrew again so as to avoid becoming infected.

The Fall of Athens

Soon afterward, Sparta and Athens signed a truce that stopped the war for a while, but it wasn't long before they were back to their old ways. Athens lost a bunch of men and ships in a disastrous expedition to Sicily, and the Spartans ended up building their own fleet.

In the same year, 430 BC, the Athenian ships, which were caught in a **storm**, were forced to take refuge on a beach near Sparta. When the Spartans realized that the Athenian ships were stranded and helpless on the sand, they attacked the sailors and set fire to the ships.

Without a fleet to bring food to the city and protect its allies, Athens was forced to **surrender**.

Sparta's allies wanted to raze Athens to the ground and sell its inhabitants into slavery, but the Spartans, remembering Athens' victories during the war against the Persians, refused.

Socrates (470-399 BC) was one of the most interesting figures to emerge in Athens during this period. The son of a sculptor, he immediately stood out for his **intelligence**. He was a brave soldier in combat and took part in many of the battles in the Peloponnese War. When his father died, Socrates was able to live on the money that he had been left, and he devoted himself to teaching. He became famous as a **teacher** and many important people sent their children to study with him.

Socrates' classes were different from those of other teachers. Instead of talking, Socrates asked questions, forcing his pupils to think and come to their own conclusions. This rhetorical method was later called the **Socratic method**.

Socrates never wrote anything down, but he had a pupil who did. His name was Aristocles, and he was a professional wrestler, but everyone called him **Plato**, meaning "the wide," because of his broad shoulders. Plato's texts describe Socrates talking to friends and pupils on subjects such as law, justice, love, and friendship.

YOU MAY NOT KNOW THAT...
Socrates was married to a woman named **Xanthippe**. She was said to be as much of a **genius** as her husband, but Socrates' pupils described her as a bossy woman with a very bad temper.

The story goes that, after a terrible argument, Xanthippe threw a chamber pot at her husband's head. Covered in pee, Socrates said, "After the thunder comes the rain."

The Death of Socrates

The Spartans left Athens in the charge of a series of corrupt rulers who became known as the **Thirty Tyrants**. It didn't take the Athenians long to rebel, and after expelling them, they restored democracy.

When they realized that some of these hated tyrants had been Socrates' pupils, they took him to **court** on charges of offending the gods and teaching anti-democratic ideas. Instead of asking for forgiveness, he faced up to the judges and constantly used the Socratic method to defend himself. The judges were angry and condemned him to death—in reality, however, what they wanted was for him to **leave** the city, so they locked him in a cell that he could easily escape from. But he was old and tired, so he decided to set an example of obedience to the law. He talked with his friends and pupils all night, and at dawn, he complied with the sentence and drank the **poison** that killed him.

After the defeat of Athens, Sparta became the **dominant power** in Greece. Many cities had to accept Spartan rulers, who were outright thieves. The democracies that had triumphed, supported by the Athenians, were replaced by **oligarchies**. In this scenario, many cities revolted against Sparta.

In 371 BC, the Spartans decided to teach a lesson to the important city of **Thebes**, so that it could serve as an example to the others. Relying on their reputation for invincibility, they attacked the Theban forces, who were led by a brilliant general named **Epaminondas** (418-362 BC). The battle was to take place in the fields next to the village of **Leuctra**.

Epaminondas thought up a plan to compensate for the Spartans' superiority. It consisted of **concentrating** his best troops in one specific spot, even at the risk of weakening other parts of his formation. The plan worked, the Spartan phalanx broke, and many soldiers died, including the Spartan king **Cleombrotus I**. It was the first time that the Spartans had been defeated in open battle. With its prestige in tatters, Sparta lost control of Greece forever. Ruined by continuous wars, Spartans began to leave the Peloponnese to seek work as mercenaries in other areas.

Sparta tried to defeat the Thebans once more in 362 BC at the **Battle of Mantinea**. Epaminondas' tactics again

led to Sparta's defeat, but before losing the battle, the Spartans gave the order to kill Epaminondas. A spear struck down the brilliant Theban general, and with this came the end of Thebes' victories. The Greek cities would again clash with each other, unaware that a new enemy lurked from the north: **Macedonia** and Philip's time had come.

MACEDONIA'S TIME COMES:
PHILIP

Philip II (382-336 BC) was heir to the kingdom of **Macedonia**, a region in northern Greece that many Greeks considered a land of barbarians and savages. When he was very young, he was sent to Thebes, where he received military training from Epaminondas himself.

When he returned to Macedonia and seized power, he began to reorganize the army. He made his subjects into **professional soldiers**: As they were paid a salary, they were no longer dependent on their crops and didn't need to return home at the end of the summer. The king provided them with helmets, armor, and a huge spear that was up to twenty-three feet long called a **sarisa**. In addition to this main body of hoplites, his army had a highly effective **cavalry** and a light **infantry** corps for sieges. Philip began to put his plan into action: It involved nothing less than the total **conquest** of Greece.

IF YOU WANT SOMETHING DONE PROPERLY, DO IT *YOURSELF*.

YOU MAY NOT KNOW THAT...
During the siege of the city of Methone, an **arrow** pierced Philip's eye.

His doctors took the arrow out, but the wound became infected. The only thing they could do was completely empty the **eye** socket, but Philip was known for his bad temper, so no doctor dared to do it.

Philip took a dessert **spoon** and gouged out his eye himself. From then on, he would be known as **Philip the One Eye**.

Macedonia began to conquer Greek cities one after the other, taking advantage of the fact that they were all fighting with each other. However, there came a time when the Greeks realized what was going on. They organized a gigantic army with troops from Athens and Thebes, and they confronted Philip in 338 BC at the **Battle of Chaeronea**.

The Macedonian soldiers, led by Philip, defeated the Greek hoplites while his cavalry, commanded by his son **Alexander**, defeated the enemy's cavalry.

After conquering Greece, Philip thought about using his formidable army to attack the Persian Empire. While finalizing plans for the invasion, he attended a religious ceremony in a crowded theater. There, in front of everyone, one of his bodyguards drew his sword and killed him. The assassin died while trying to get away, and it was never known who was behind the attack.

One of the various rumors was that it was the work of Philip's wife and Alexander's mother, Queen **Olympias**. Philip had recently separated from her to marry a younger woman; Olympias was proud and didn't take well to the new situation. Philip's death was good news for her son, **Alexander**, because he was proclaimed king on the spot.

Alexander the Great (356-323 BC) was a fascinating, intelligent character with boundless self-confidence. He was Philip and Olympias' eldest son, and he grew up surrounded by other high-class Macedonian boys who became his generals and all were taught by the famous philosopher **Aristotle**.

The story goes that when he was ten years old, he managed to tame a horse called **Bucephalus**, which everyone thought was untamable. Alexander realized that the horse was afraid of his shadow and made him face into the sun so that he couldn't see it. His father told him that he would have to find another kingdom, because Macedonia was too small for him. Over the years, Alexander became a good horseman and officer, but he was also a rebellious teenager, and Philip threw him out of the house on several occasions.

At the age of **twenty**, he was proclaimed king after his father's assassination. When the **Thebans** heard of Philip's death, they decided to revolt, but the Macedonian army was an efficient war machine, and they didn't stand a chance. Alexander defeated them, destroyed Thebes, and sold the survivors into slavery. He decided to carry on with his father's plans and landed in Persia at the head of his army, a troop of veteran soldiers who had conquered Greece and were about to **conquer the world**.

The Conquest of Asia

Alexander defeated the Persians in a couple of battles and conquered several **coastal cities** to provide ports for the transport of troops and supplies. He conquered the various kingdoms of the Persian Empire until he reached Egypt, where he was proclaimed **Pharaoh**. In 331 BC, he had a city built there in his name. This was **Alexandria**, which was destined to become one of the most important cities in the ancient world.

The Persian king, **Darius**, saw his empire being conquered rapidly, so he decided to stake everything on a single battle in which he himself would lead his army. He chose a wide plain near a village called **Gaugamela**.

Darius planned to overwhelm the Macedonians using **chariots** equipped with swords at their sides—but Alexander's veterans were expecting something along these lines. During the fighting, they left open corridors and killed the chariot drivers as they passed. Alexander concentrated his forces on attacking the king in person. A cavalry charge supported by heavy infantry pushed its way through the elite troops protecting him. When Darius saw Alexander advancing toward him, he left the battlefield in his chariot, followed by his personal guard. As soon as the other Persians realized that the king had fled, they **surrendered** en masse.

Alexander in India

Alexander pursued Darius across Asia, incorporating the various kingdoms of the Persian Empire into his own. When Darius' trusted men saw that all was lost, they **murdered** their king and fled. But since Alexander wanted to not only conquer the world but also **unite** it, he took the Persians into his arm, rather than enslaving them or destroying their cities.

On his advance eastward, he entered India in 326 BC. He conquered smaller cities and kingdoms until he reached present-day Pakistan and encountered the army of King **Porus**, who was unlike any other king he had faced. Porus personally led a charge of **fifty war elephants**. The Macedonians had never seen elephants before, and many were crushed to death as they tried to flee. Alexander was nearly defeated for the first time, but his veterans held out. They dodged the arrows, fought their way to the Indians' rear, and surrounded them from behind. Alexander's horse, Bucephalus, was killed by an Indian spear. Alexander ordered a city to be built on the spot where he had fallen: **Bucephala**.

After this battle, Alexander and his troops arrived on the banks of the River **Ganges**, one of the greatest rivers in the world. On the other side of the river, the Macedonian soldiers saw a huge Indian army which was much larger than that of Porus, with thousands of elephants. The soldiers told Alexander that they didn't intend to cross the river and asked to return home. He had no choice but to return to Persia, but he did so by a different route than the one they had taken, through one of the hottest and driest places on the planet: the **Gedrosian Desert**. Such a great number of soldiers died of thirst there that many thought it was a punishment for being unwilling to follow Alexander to the end of the world.

Alexander settled in **Babylon**. He began to make plans to unite his vast domains: roads linking Africa and Europe, cities with European and Asian populations, and huge fleets that would conquer the Mediterranean. However, none of these plans would ever come to fruition. Alexander died mysteriously at the age of thirty-two, leaving behind a life of legend .

GREAT REWARD FOR TWENTY-FIVE YEARS OF SERVICE...

AN ALL-EXPENSES PAID TRIP THROUGH A *DESERT*.

The Diadochi

The men that were closest to Alexander were his **generals**—unfortunately, they didn't share his vision of a united world. They just wanted to rule, and he got on their nerves, so it's pretty likely that they **poisoned** Alexander and his best friend, General Hephaestion.

These generals were called the **Diadochi**, which means "successors" in Greek. They fought each other a series of wars that lasted for many years. The three most successful among them were **Seleucus**, who took Asia, **Antigonus**, who took Greece and Macedonia, and **Ptolemy**, ancestor of the famous Cleopatra, who took Egypt and founded what is known as the Ptolemaic dynasty.

The point is that, by the time of his death in 323 BC, Alexander had created a huge empire and had taken **Greek culture** farther than anyone before him.

To some he was a conqueror, to others a tyrant. However, his exploits and travels made him a legendary figure, and he started to become known as Alexander the Great.

THE HELLENISTIC PERIOD

4th-1st Centuries BC

Hellenism is the period of Greek history from Alexander the Great's death to Cleopatra's suicide. The Greek cities that had dominated the Classical Period, such as Athens or Sparta, were no longer important. Kingdoms and cities larger than those in classical Greece emerged on top of the ruins of the vanished Persian Empire. There, writers, artists, and scientists would have access to **resources** and wealth that were unthinkable until then. Legendary **libraries**, gigantic **statues**, and incredible **scientific** advances mark this period. But since the Greeks were always very fond of killing each other, these times were no different in that respect. The continuous wars between them greatly weakened the Hellenistic kingdoms, and it was easy for the **Romans** to conquer them one by one.

A MAN NAMED PTOLEMY

Ptolemy (367-283 BC) was the son of a Macedonian nobleman and grew up in the Palace of Pella with Alexander the Great and some of his other generals. He accompanied Alexander on all his campaigns and was appointed admiral of the Macedonian navy. After his leader's death, Ptolemy was appointed **Governor of Egypt**.

During the Wars of the Diadochi, his power spread to several islands in the Mediterranean. At the end of the conflict, he proclaimed himself **Pharaoh** and ruled Egypt from **Alexandria**, a city founded by Alexander on the shores of the Mediterranean. It would eventually replace Athens as the **cultural capital** of the Greek world.

Ptolemy made Alexandria the most important port in the Mediterranean. With all the money that flowed into the city, he was able to finance some really iconic **projects**. Ptolemy's descendants, the **Ptolemaic dynasty**, ruled Egypt for the next three hundred years.

The Lighthouse of Alexandria

Just opposite the harbor, there was a small, rocky islet called **Pharos**. Ptolemy ordered a huge tower to be built there, and at the top, he had **mirrors** installed that reflected the light from the sun during the day and from a huge bonfire at night.

The light from the lighthouse guided **ships** safely to the harbor entrance. It was such an ingenious idea that lighthouses soon began to appear all over the Mediterranean. The Greeks of later times considered the Lighthouse of Alexandria to be one of the **Seven Wonders of the Ancient World**.

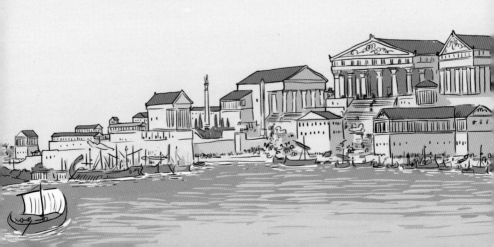

THE LIBRARY
OF ALEXANDRIA

Ptolemy was also the founder of the **Museum of Alexandria**, a kind of university dedicated to the **Muses**, the inspirational goddesses of art and literature from which we get the word "museum."

The museum housed temples, gardens, and laboratories, as well as bedchambers and a luxurious, communal dining hall. The idea was that the best poets, writers, and scientists of the ancient world would live and work together to spread Greek **culture and science** throughout the world.

The Pharaohs paid the wisest men in the Greek world to travel to Alexandria, and this led to astonishing scientific discoveries and great literary achievements. The museum held facilities of all kinds, from zoos to astronomical observatories, but the most famous was undoubtedly the library.

The Library of Alexandria

It's said that when a ship arrived in the port of Alexandria, it was meticulously searched by officials looking for **papyri**. When they found one, it was taken to the library, where a copy was made and given to its owner. The original remained in the library, which eventually held **half a million** papyri.

The library received large sums of money to make copies of the most important works of Greek thought. The works were **classified** by subject and author, and they were made available to anyone who wanted to consult them. The world would have to wait until the invention of the printing press to see so many books in one place again.

In 305 BC, **Antigonus** (382-301 BC), another of Alexander's former generals, sent his son **Demetrius** to attack the island of **Rhodes**, an ally of Ptolemy.

Demetrius used huge assault towers and other ingenious machines to try to conquer the city, but the Rhodians **flooded** the ground that the towers were advancing over, and they sank into the mud. Shortly afterward, Ptolemy's army came to his ally's aid, and Demetrius had to beat a hasty retreat, leaving behind weapons and machinery. In gratitude for saving them at the last moment, the Rhodians bestowed the title of **Soter**, or "savior," on Ptolemy.

The Colossus of Rhodes

Grateful for their victory, the Rhodians decided to erect a huge bronze sculpture dedicated to **Apollo**, the city's patron god, in 280 BC. They sold the weapons abandoned by Demetrius and used the towers as scaffolding to build the largest statue in the world. *The Colossus* was around a hundred and thirty feet high, about the same height as the Statue of Liberty (without the base), and it was considered another of the **Seven Wonders**. The sculptor who built it miscalculated the budget and ended up broke. Desperate because he couldn't pay his debts, he committed suicide.

The statue didn't stand for long. In 226 BC, fifty-four years after being built, it was toppled by an **earthquake**, and the Rhodians thought it was the gods' will, so they didn't rebuild it.

The Colossus was left lying at the entrance to the harbor as a testament to the greatness of the ancients for eight hundred years. In AD 653, the island was conquered by the **Muslims** and the bronze was sold to a merchant, who needed **nine hundred camels** to transport it.

THE END OF
THE HELLENISTIC PERIOD

After dominating Greece for three hundred years, the Macedonian Empire also came to an end. A new military power, **Rome**, was making its way across the Mediterranean, step by step. Rome attacked the Greek cities in Italy and completely defeated them.

After conquering Italy, the Romans attacked the Macedonians and fought several wars against them, in which the Roman legions faced the Macedonian phalanxes. At the **Battle of Pydna** in 168 BC, the Macedonians broke formation in pursuit of the retreating legionaries and opened their ranks too wide. The Romans turned back and penetrated the gaps in the phalanx. It was an absolute rout. By 146 BC, Greece and Macedonia had become **Roman provinces**.

Cleopatra, the Last of the Ptolemaic Dynasty

In 48 BC, **Julius Caesar** landed in Egypt, where the king's two children, **Cleopatra VII** (69-30 BC) and Ptolemy XIII, were fighting a civil war. Caesar was supposed to make peace between the two, but Cleopatra is said to have snuck into his palace at night by hiding in a laundry basket, and the two became lovers.

When Julius Caesar was assassinated, his general **Mark Antony** married Cleopatra, but Caesar's nephew, Augustus, defeated them both at the **Battle of Actium** in 31 BC. Egypt became a Roman province and Cleopatra, Ptolemy's last descendant, committed suicide a few months later. The Hellenistic world had ended, and a period of Greek history marked by Roman domination began.

THE END OF
THE HELLENISTIC PERIOD

The Roman conquest didn't stop **Greek culture**. The victorious generals brought Greek paintings, statues, and vases to Rome that were very successful. In fact, after the conquest, Greek culture became fashionable among high-class Romans who commissioned copies of Greek books, statues, and paintings to decorate their villas. In the markets, large sums exchanged hands for Greek slaves who were highly sought-after as teachers. All educated Romans spoke and read both Greek and Latin.

The Roman poet **Horace** wrote: *Graecia capta ferum victorem cepit*, which means, "In being conquered, Greece herself conquered her ferocious conqueror."

But all this love for Greek culture turned to hate when the **Christians** came to power. It should be borne in mind that Greek culture was expressed through its **polytheistic religion**: Sculptures depicted Olympian gods, sporting competitions were considered sacred, and in the theater, the gods often appeared on stage to assist the main characters. Even science and philosophy were surrounded by an unmistakable whiff of **paganism**.

As a result, the bishops declared **war on the culture** that sustained this religion. They demolished temples and statues, mutilated reliefs, tore down frescoes and mosaics, burned libraries, cut down sacred groves, and scraped clean parchments containing classical texts to write prayers on them instead.

Christian religious fanaticism wasn't limited to art and science.

The case of **Hypatia of Alexandria** is an example of what happened throughout the entire Roman Empire. Hypatia was a very famous mathematician. She wrote books on calculus, geometry, and astronomy, and she taught at the Museum of Alexandria. Her pupils included influential members of the Roman government, some of whom were Christians, who had great admiration and respect for her, but none of this was enough to save her.

In AD 415, possibly on the orders of **Bishop Cyril of Alexandria**, a fanatical mob attacked Hypatia and dragged her out of the carriage in which she was travelling. Hypatia was tortured and murdered in public. Cyril is revered as a saint by the Catholic, Orthodox, Coptic, and Lutheran Churches.

The Destruction of the Library of Alexandria

A Christian rabble attacked the Museum of Alexandria and **set fire to the library**.

All that scientific and literary knowledge was reduced to ashes and lost forever. Alexandria ceased to be the center of knowledge, and Greek science came to an end.

One by one, the symbols of Greek culture disappeared, destroyed by Christian intolerance. The **Olympic Games** were held for the last time in the year 393. They were then banned by an edict of the Roman Emperor **Theodosius** after twelve centuries of existence. The great statue of Zeus, which Phidias had sculpted eight centuries earlier, was removed, and it was destroyed by fire in 476.

The final blow came in 529, when Emperor Justinian closed the **Academy of Athens**, founded by Plato nine centuries earlier. The philosophy teachers were forced to leave for Persia, and the last trace of pre-Christian Greek life was erased for all time.

THE LEGACY
OF THE GREEKS

The ancient Greeks created the most **fascinating and influential** civilization in world history. In order to attack their gods and the classical culture they represented, Christians ended up destroying much more than works of art.

After the triumph of Christianity, Europe was plunged into a **dark age** of religious fanaticism and superstition. Scientific advances were forgotten, Greek **medicine**—the most advanced in the world at the time—was banned, and the women who knew about it were called witches and murdered.

Christians and Muslims strove to **erase** every vestige of Greek civilization. The temples that had been left standing were demolished and looted, marble sculptures and reliefs were destroyed to make lime, and bronze statues were melted down for their metal.

As time went on, only a few **ruins** remained as witnesses to the most interesting culture in antiquity. Indeed, when Europe rediscovered the legacy of classical civilization, the Middle Ages ended, and the **Renaissance** began.

A few centuries later, Europeans rediscovered the **scientific method**, which enabled them to develop the technology with which they conquered the world. This method was created by **Thales**, one of the greatest geniuses of the ancient world, in a small Ionian city called Miletus.

The Greeks were an interesting and curious people, being lovers of beauty and pleasure, but also of learning and doing things properly. They had their faults, of course: Slavery was wrong, whichever way you look at it. But the idea of citizens having the right to decide their own destiny and not having to bow down before any king, tyrant, or priest was born and developed in that little place called **Greece**.

And we have to be grateful to them for that.

Illustrated History
for Kids and Teenagers

ROME
THE VIKINGS
ANCIENT GREECE

Available soon...

THE INCAS
ANCIENT EGYPT

LOOK, WE'RE CIVILIZED FOLK IN THIS PLACE: WHEN WE DRINK OUT OF OUR ENEMIES' SKULLS, WE USE COASTERS.

THE LEGIONS OF ROME

THE EXPEDITIONS OF THE VIKINGS

THE OLYMPIC GAMES OF GREECE

Available soon...

THE GOLD OF THE INCAS

ILLUSTRATED HISTORY - ANCIENT GREECE
First edition: February 2024

© Text and illustrations: Miguel Ángel Saura, 2024
© Translated from Spanish by Carolyn Louise Black.
© Editorial el Pirata, 2024
Sabadell (Barcelona)
info@editorialelpirata.com
www.editorialelpirata.com

FSC
www.fsc.org
100%
From well-
managed forests
FSC® C152346

All rights reserved
ISBN: 978-84-19898-11-1
Legal deposit: B 18505-2023
Printed in China

With support from